FOR

I THINK YOU'D ENJOY THIS BOOK BECAUSE

FROM

PRINCIPLES FOR THE NEXT CENTURY OF WORK

Sense & Respond Press publishes short, beautiful, actionable books on topics related to innovation, digital transformation, product management, and design. Our readers are smart, busy, practical innovators. Our authors are experts working in the fields they write about.

The goal of every book in our series is to solve a real-world problem for our readers. Whether that be understanding a complex and emerging topic, or something as concrete (and difficult) as hiring innovation leaders, our books help working professionals get better at their jobs, quickly.

Jeff Gothelf & Josh Seiden

Series co-editors **Jeff Gothelf** and **Josh Seiden** wrote *Lean UX* (O'Reilly) and *Sense & Respond* (Harvard Business Review Press) together. They were co-founding Principals of Neo Innovation (sold to Pivotal Labs) in New York City and helped build it into one of the most recognized brands in modern product strategy, development, and design. In 2017 they were short-listed for the Thinkers50 award for their contributions to innovation leadership. Learn more about Jeff and Josh at www.jeffgothelf.com and www.joshseiden.com.

INVISIBLE LEADER

Issued in print and electronic formats.

ISBN 978-1-0996085-5-1 (KDP paperback)

Editor: Victoria Olsen
Designer: Mimi O Chun
Interior typesetting: Jennifer Blais

Published in the United States by Sense & Respond Press
www.senseandrespondpress.com

Printed and bound in the United States.
1 2 3 4   22 21 20 19

Elena Astilleros

INVISIBLE LEADER

Facilitation secrets for catalyzing
change, cultivating innovation, and
commanding results

SENSE &
RESPOND
PRESS

INTRODUCTION: BECOMING INVISIBLE

The business of doing business is changing.
Product deliveries whiz by at mind boggling speeds,
organizations steadily hack away at traditional
structures, and the question "what are we going
to do about the millennials?" lingers in the halls.
Facilitation skills provide a lightweight framework for
leading and making sense of these changes.

Though facilitative skills apply to more than just meetings, this book uses meetings as a vehicle to highlight them. There are three main reasons for this:

1. Meetings are a common recurrence in our schedules and have clear start and end times.

2. We feel a natural urgency to improve our meetings and have ample opportunities to iterate on the process.

3. Facilitative skills learned in running meetings are transferable outside of them.

Given the massive amount of time we spend in meetings, it seems as if we should have them down to a science. Unfortunately, some of us pull them off better than others. Consider the following situations:

Situation 1:

Jack, the brilliant Vice President of a well-known Fortune 500 company, surveyed the stark, nearly lethargic boardroom. His jaw clenched. People were starting to check out. Earlier, his group had asked questions of such a tactical and specific nature that they annoyed him. Now, though the tactical questions had stopped, so had any other questions.

Situation 2:

Mariana, Jack's unassuming peer, was beaming as she reflected and responded to her group's dynamics. Her latest workshop was a bastion of activity: people were rotating around the room to ask each other questions, posting sticky notes, and even smiling.

Earlier, her group had voiced confusion and anxiety about the work ahead of them, and in response Mariana both asked and answered questions. Now, participants were working together as if their confusion never existed.

Jack's meeting follows a traditional leadership model. Mariana's reveals the opportunities created by facilitative leadership. As these two scenarios illustrate, meetings either waste time or produce greatness, and each of these outcomes has implications for future employee performance. Therefore, when a meeting looks like Jack's, the time investment is not the only loss. People who go on autopilot in a meeting pick up the habit of going on autopilot elsewhere, which ultimately affects the organization's bottom line.

In a meeting like Mariana's, participants engage, find creative solutions to their problems, and look back on the results with pride. They are also motivated to maintain their productivity long after the meeting is over, and after enough of these experiences, a work culture develops that improves the bottom line.

But just how does one create this kind of success?

According to the leadership models of old, the answer to that question is that you gather a talented team and take a hardline position in relating to them. However, Tom Peters and Robert Waterman disproved that model in their decades old classic, *In Search of Excellence*. Referring to Frederic Taylor, who originated the concept behind scientific management (the task optimization model of assembly-line production), they wrote, "the central problem with the rationalist view of organizing people is that people are not very rational. To fit Taylor's old model, or today's organizational charts, man is simply designed wrong." So, what's the real secret?

It's the power of **invisible leadership**. Peters and Waterman later write in the same book, "leadership is many things. . . being visible when things go awry, and invisible when they are working well."

At its best, facilitative leadership catalyzes change, cultivates innovation, and commands results, but it cannot be seen by the naked eye. Using two archetypal leaders, we will put a lens on invisibility, and show how it differs from traditional management.

As you read, keep in mind that facilitative leadership is something you do before, during, and after meetings. This continuity can make it seem ordinary instead of effortful, to the point where you rarely seem to lead at all. In fact, as Lyssa Adkins writes in *Coaching Agile Teams*, this is the type of leadership that, if "done well, is impossible to see from outside the team and can be invisible even to the team members."

Now, how do you become invisible?

The answer to that question lies in this book.

LAYING THE FOUNDATION

Invisible leadership begins with a strong foundation in the principles of new management frameworks like positive leadership, liberation management, and adaptive leadership. These people-centered approaches change the game of business from one of fighting not to lose, to one of win/win. I'll include links to helpful resources on these topics in the Reading List at the end of the book. In this chapter, we will discuss the common features of these management approaches: **practicing neutrality, setting context,** and **championing team members**.

To Jack, the team is only valuable insofar as it produces a victory. If anyone on his team seems like a weak link, he rips them to shreds—sometimes to the point of public humiliation. And when team members want to celebrate their victories, he grows impatient. After all, they're "supposed" to be victorious. The result of Jack's negative reactions is that his staff is less willing to engage.

By contrast, Mariana views her work relationships as life long, so she focuses on building rapport. She strives to ensure that every team member feels supported, because she thinks that strong teams create strong products. And when she sees someone demonstrate growth, she's ecstatic to highlight their transformation. As a result, Mariana's staff is eager to put forth their best.

If Mariana's approach seems too 'touchy-feely' for the archetypal workplace, that's understandable. After all, we often think of the business world as a place where rational thinking reigns supreme and focusing on feelings is useless. That being said, invisible leaders know the truth: great creations are messy, unpredictable, and yes, even irrational. By accepting chaos instead of ignoring it, they build environments where their teams can flourish regardless. In their book, *Primal Leadership*, Daniel Goleman, Richard Boyatzis, and Annie McKee argue that "great leadership works through the emotions" and that the "fundamental task of leaders . . . is to prime good feelings in those they lead." They describe how a leader, "manages meaning for a group, offering a way to interpret or make sense of, and so react emotionally to, a given situation."

By using the principles in this chapter, leaders can establish a radically different relationship with their team members and meeting participants and create the conditions where team members feel respected, safe, and ready to apply their talent in new and fascinating ways.

PRACTICE NEUTRALITY

In science, neutrality means having no inherent positive or negative charge, but in business, neutrality means *safety*. The researchers behind the Aristotle Project, Google's multi-year initiative to hack into the secrets of high performing teams, found that safety is the most important dynamic in an effective team.

It is important to recognize the depth of care it takes to be neutral. In their study, *Making the Case for Employee Resource Groups,* Theresa M. Wellbourne and Lacey Leone McLaughlin write:

> "In most organizations, there exist built-in barriers to innovation. Hierarchy, punishment for risk taking, fear of not fitting in. . . and peer pressure all make excellent environments for stopping innovative ideas from being communicated and executed."

Practicing neutrality mitigates resistance to innovation so that members have the courage to propose and act on out-of-the-box ideas.

Being neutral does not equal being robotic. In practicing neutrality, a leader must doggedly commit to an outcome, yet stay unattached to the solution. He or she must also have enough wisdom to distinguish between judgement and discernment. To discern means to perceive, recognize, comprehend, and notice the differences and distinctions from one topic to another. To judge is to pass a sentence on another person or idea. That is the last thing we want to encourage as facilitators. This difference keeps meetings generative, yet safe from falling down too many rabbit holes. It also protects innovative ideas (which often start off unpopular) from brash judgements of the group

Analyn Nouri, VP of Software at Ticketmaster, practices neutrality even during the tough times. "Even if it hurts," she says, "you have to be honest. It's easy and cowardly to sugar coat. It's like military training: if you are going to lead your team to death, have the courage to tell them what you're doing, but be there with them."

To practice neutrality in a meeting:

» Identify any bias that would alter the outcome of the meeting, then identify a plan to handle that bias. For example, you might have strong feelings about the issues or stakeholders that you're discussing. Or perhaps, you know that the team feels strongly about a topic. Simply sharing the bias with meeting attendees helps with neutralization.

» Ask participants to share their opinions of an idea before sharing your own. Perhaps your team wants to implement a new workflow, and you already 'know' which one will provide the best results. Hear the opinion of the attendees and repeat back what you hear the group sharing. This level of facilitation often makes it easier for you to change your mind when a better solution arises. Recuse yourself if you find you are simply too charged on the topic to accept new information shared by your team.

» Stand in a neutral position, similar to the ready position of an athlete. Limber body, with open hands, and alert eyes. This position allows your brain to take in more information, while quickly responding to that information. For example, when someone in the meeting introduces crucial new details, taking a neutral position allows the facilitator to quickly assimilate new data without conveying judgement. This is quite different from adopting a accusatory posture and annoyed expression, as if to convey a sentiment of "why didn't you say this sooner?!"

SET CONTEXT

The word context originally meant to join by weaving. Leaders weave atmospheres that influence the behaviors of others through subtle and unwritten cues. As a result, people would behave differently in the presence of Jeff Bezos than they would in front of Oprah Winfrey.

Invisible leaders are never simply one person. They shift and morph to adapt to their environment. Bill Walsh, champion coach of the San Francisco 49ers football team, mastered this art when his players were especially glum about their results. Walsh became the quintessential invisible leader when he traded places with a bell hop and helped the team when they arrived at a hotel. It wasn't until he got into a luggage-fueled tug of war with Joe Montana, his star quarterback, that the players realized who their bellhop really was. This caused the entire team to erupt in laughter and changed the whole mood of the group.

Asking yourself the following questions can help determine how you set context:

» What's the current mood of the team right now?
» What kind of mood do I want to set?
» What kind of leadership do I need to bring to set that mood?

In his article, *Leading Change*, John Kotter argues that not establishing a great enough sense of urgency causes major change initiatives to fail. Invisible leaders address this by setting the context of urgency. Setting context speaks to how you want people to act around you. In subsequent chapters we will review setting the mood and preparing in advance of the meeting.

CHAMPION TEAM MEMBERS

To champion means to fight. Championing team members means operating as if their success were a foregone conclusion. It also means respecting everyone in a meeting equally, whether that person is a team member or a C suite executive. This creates an even distribution of authority within the group and neutralizes potential power plays caused by favoritism.

CEO of Quality Works Consulting Group, Stacy Kirk knows how to champion her teams. She knows they help her work smarter and not harder, so she listens in order to quickly pinpoint their best qualities. In assigning a team member to a task, she shares her regard for their abilities as the reason for the assignment, "I'm assigning you to research this task because you're a learner." When the occasional failure befalls a team member, she reminds them, as stated in an interview with Paul Stennett, that "failure is part of the process and . . . on the other side of failure are many more opportunities to win." Kirk dares her team members to think even bigger, and her winning smile communicates her faith and nurtures their confidence. As a result, her team members feel comfortable taking bolder risks, going the extra mile, and knowing they can win even after a setback. Years after working with her, team members remember those days as some of the best in their career.

Elements of a basic championing experience in a meeting:
  » Eye contact
  » Smiling
  » Using a person's name while speaking to them
  » Listening with care and high regard

» Respecting the person's ability and natural talent
» Verbalizing trust in their potential for solving tough problems
» Appreciating their participation

When Taiichi Ohno and Eiji Toyoda established the Toyota Production System, they linked *reducing waste* to *revitalizing Japan.* This focus allowed them to challenge their workforce when they noticed idleness. Because Taiichi Ohno encouraged an atmosphere of efficiency, respect, and honor, workers didn't feel criticized. Rather, they felt like champions of their country.

PREPARING

Preparing before a meeting allows facilitators to set and communicate their expectations to their team. Teams, in turn, can confidently collaborate together because they know what they need to do to succeed. In this chapter, we'll discuss three tools of effective preparation: **defining value**, **priming guests**, and **coordinating logistics**.

Jack's schedule never permits him much time to prepare for meetings. Therefore, his invites simply contain time and location or video conference information. At the meeting start, Jack sets up while everyone waits. This results in invitees who often have no clue what's at stake, aren't sure when they should speak up, and when they do talk, spend much of the time rehashing the same questions or requesting fresh whiteboard markers.

Mariana's attitude towards preparation is that it's essential and time-saving. Therefore, if she has a big meeting scheduled on Wednesday, she starts preparing for it on Tuesday, even if it that means arranging a pre-meeting with her leaders and stocking up on conference room supplies. When sending her invites, she keeps in mind that her invitees excel at what they do, thus they always have more demands for their skills than time to meet them. For that reason, her invites reflect why the meeting is worthwhile and the invitees' contributions necessary. Finally, she manages her schedule and strives to arrive at her meetings early. The result of this is that her team is convinced of her commitment and responds to her in kind by coming ready to work toward a goal they're all invested in.

We can look at preparing as similar to the primary step in the *discovery/planning* phase of the software development life cycle. In Japan, preparation is seen as so crucial that there is a special name for the process: *nemawashi*. With nemawashi, leaders of a change build consensus for their work by broadly sharing their plan, most critically with the groups affected by their change, and by addressing any concerns that surround the work.

The amount of preparing a facilitator needs to do depends on the amount of investment the meeting requires. Larger changes require more preparation, while small changes need minimal preparation. For instance, as a lightweight preparation for meetings, former United States Secretary of Defense Robert Gates would take off his blazer, to help meeting attendees feel more comfortable approaching him. In the inevitable moment that meetings start without time for preparation, invisible leaders let their teams know the reason for the lack of preparation.

DEFINE VALUE

Define value by measuring against two factors: other work which could have been completed at the same time, and the opportunity cost to the organization should the meeting not happen. When the outcome of the meeting does not exceed the value of other work that could be completed in the same time, do not call the meeting. Instead, look for a different way to solve the problem.

Both the Lean Startup and Agile movements stress defining value as a core tenet to delivering great products. Facilitative leaders extend this practice into their everyday leadership style. When asking anything of their teams, they not only define the problem they want solved and why it matters, they also ask:

1. What value will participants gain?

2. What would create, build, and maintain the excitement for the work?

3. What will indicate success?

4. What will constitute a pivot?

5. Who needs to be invited?

Creating excitement often receives less importance than outcomes, pivots, and success, yet, it is crucial for innovation and productivity. David Sousa explains in *How the Brain Learns* that positive environments foster the release of endorphins in the brain that increase learning and creative capacities. Creating excitement makes team members want to return and contribute great work. During a resilience engineering meetup in Los Angeles, John Allspaw, former CTO at Etsy, shared that Etsy facilitators designed their postmortem debriefs so that participants would want to come back. This attention to meeting dynamics helped build the Etsy debriefing culture to a point where participants arrived early, and the popularity of some debriefs led to standing-room only attendance. This also led the facilitators to document their best practices and create trainings so that others could replicate their results.

Invisible leaders have a knack for getting funding for innovative research. This is because they show the value of the investment in a holistic manner and highlight opportunity costs, such as effects to future organic top-line growth to help funders agree to back their projects.

PRIME GUESTS

Priming guests prepares them for what's expected in the meeting ahead. Priming begins with the meeting invite and continues with *follow ups*, *teasers*, and *interviews*.

Invitation titles set meetings in motion. In "We've Got to Stop Meeting Like This: Tips for Better Workplace Gatherings,"

Priya Parker asks leaders to thoughtfully title their meeting: "'Is it a sales meeting?' or a 'How to Crush It This Quarter Meeting?'" Details like these build the excitement for the meeting. When you look back at these invites, which meeting would *you* rather attend?

Extend the title's tone to the subject of the invite. Share the value of the meeting, why invitees were selected, a rough plan for the meeting and what you hope attendees walk away with.

> *I've created bonus content for this book that includes example invitations you can customize. See Reading List at the end of this book for the link.*

After sending the invite, keep the meeting attendees engaged through follow ups, teasers, and interviews. Keep in mind, 100% participation rarely happens with follow ups, teasers, or interviews. Think of them as hype, or tools to build the excitement of the group.

Follow Ups

Follow up individually with some meeting participants. Hallway conversations, chat rooms, and standups offer an easy way to remind them of the meeting. Transfer the tone of your invites to your follow ups. If you've invited participants to *crush it,* keep that same energy by using that tone throughout your preparation.

Teasers

Teasers arouse interest in the upcoming meeting and their forms can vary from an email to a verbal "heads up" or open challenge on the wall, e.g. "if we needed to reduce waste in our organization by 25% this quarter, how would we do it?" Ordinarily, teasers best serve their purpose when sent a couple of days before the meeting.

However, they can serve their purpose even within ten minutes of a meeting's start, as long as participants have time to consume their content.

Interviews

Interviews are incredibly powerful tools for preparation. Design, product, and user experience professionals perform them with stakeholders and, as a result, develop much better products. Yet few people have adapted them to facilitate better meetings. Interviews expose the needs and desires of participants and stakeholders which, when met, create results that stand out, and foster a positive outcome and outlook towards the work. The answers prepare both meeting participants and the meeting leader to make the most effective use of their time together; for instance, the leader may realize that everyone has a different mission and objective for the outcome of the meeting and, after interviewing, the leader can send follow ups to clearly state the meeting's objective.

Interviews are held prior to a meeting, either before or after drafting the agenda, and facilitators can make them as formal or informal as the meeting necessitates. The interviewing process involves asking individuals, or sometimes groups of individuals, some discovery questions to understand the lay of the land prior to the meeting. Meetings or workshops lasting a day or more should absolutely have an interview process prior to the start of the meeting. For shorter meetings, like fifteen minute huddles, the interview process can take a very informal tone, such as asking questions periodically in hallways or right before the meeting starts.

Just as a user experience professional would do in a stakeholder interview, a facilitative leader asks a selection of meeting participants questions like:

» What do you see as the purpose of the meeting?
» What questions do you need answered in this meeting?
» What should we do now to ensure success?
» What might block a successful outcome?
» What do you think I should know before conducting this meeting?

Look for patterns in the answers participants give. Again, these can highlight areas of misaligned expectations, such as who team members think is accountable for a body of work, to address before the meeting. When time does not allow for full interviews, surveys can generate similar data, and as an added bonus, sending the results of the survey to the group provides additional priming for the meeting.

Priming helps teams when they get stuck. Using metaphors to frame the problem and asking out of the box questions allows individuals to see it differently. The time between when the teaser challenges the group and when they meet also allows nascent ideas to incubate and take form.

COORDINATE LOGISTICS

A prepared physical space enhances the professionalism of a meeting and supports the participant's flow of thoughts. The next time you pass an empty conference room, step inside. What do you feel? Have you considered what it signals to your meeting participants? The look of a meeting changes the approach participants take toward it. Seemingly minor details like the legibility of materials can influence how hard or easy tasks appear to complete.

Make time to set up: test the electronic connections, clean up, reconfigure chairs, and post the materials you need to get the meeting running. Materials like an agenda, ground rules and clocks let the team know what to expect. When participants see sticky notes and markers on their desk and flip charts on the wall, they can anticipate the type of work they will tackle. Multi-textured materials that appeal to more than one sense, like scented markers, stickers, and rubber chickens, stimulate more of the brain, enhance lateral thinking, and produce better problem solving.

Note taker, time keeper, and handout distributor are all key roles to fill. Invite participants to fill them. Use their strengths to build new roles. If someone is a process expert, have them whiteboard the team's value chain.

Logistics apply to more than just meetings. They also apply to *how* a team meets, prioritizes their work, communicates internally and externally, and escalates their issues. Coordinating logistics with a team makes it easier for them to perform their work and function throughout their project.

CONDUCTING

Conducting is the act of guiding a meeting in progress. Since invisible leaders know that time is irreplaceable, they want their meeting participants to have an affirmative answer to the question "was my time well spent?" The guidance tools in this chapter help ensure participants answer this question with a resounding "yes." In this chapter, readers will learn to **define meeting moments**, as well as specific ways to **read the room** to understand the unspoken dynamics. We will end with tools and tips for how to help meeting participants **make it theirs,** which will generate a creative flow for great ideas and results, and how you can **shift the room** to guide the focus of the group.

Jack wants his team to be invested in meeting outcomes, but repeatedly "hogs the ball" by doing work and making decisions they could have handled themselves. Uncomfortable with silence, he will speak up if he doesn't hear anyone else, and once he starts talking his cursory attempts at conducting the meeting end. When this shift in focus backfires, he does nothing to hide his irritation, and sometimes finds himself yelling at individuals in the middle of a meeting. The result is that participants feel pressured to change the course of the group, but doubt if they are capable of doing so.

Mariana makes it clear that ownership of meeting outcomes lies with the team. She does this through questions such as, "What's the first thing we need to do here?" "What options do we have?" and "How might we get to a point where we can make an informed decision?" If she has no immediate questions, she might repeat the themes in what she is hearing or make observations on what she sees happening. As far as she's concerned, she has two ears and one mouth for a reason. She allows space for silence when no one answers, knowing an intrepid voice will eventually offer a solution or ask a clarifying question. She also knows that she must be careful not to view individuals as obstacles when they disagree with her. The result is that participants feel heard, respected, and competent.

Facilitators create safe spaces for the struggle and messiness that can occur in meetings. Teams must go through a period of struggle with something challenging before they can enter flow, the peak performance state where one feels and performs best. In his book, *The Rise of Superman*, flow hacker and author Steven Kotler writes that flow occurs when someone tackles a challenge four percent greater than their current capabilities. While determining the exact measure of four percent proves nearly impossible, it helps to think of it as *just a little bit ahead* of where the team is at. Use the steps in this chapter to conduct your team to that sweet spot.

DEFINE MEETING MOMENTS

In *The Power of Moments*, Chip Heath and Dan Heath tell us, "we must learn to *think in moments,* to spot the occasions that are worthy of investment." Meetings have moments, and individuals tend to focus on only a few particular moments to rate their time. Facilitative leaders make it easier on themselves by minimizing the moments they track by dividing their meetings into three familiar parts: *Openings, Midpoints*, and *Finales.*

Openings help individuals bring their attention to the work at hand. Meetings can either start dramatically or gradually warm up the group. Facilitating an opening act engages the group and drives the importance of active participation.

Key roles of the leader here are:

1. **Engagement**–Begin with an engaging question, story, or activity. Depending on the time allotted, this can mean an icebreaker activity, or a simple question like "what outcome would you like to see happen today?"

2. **Introductions**–Share why the group has gathered and the outcomes you expect. Introduce yourself, other presenters or facilitators, and, if needed, allow the group to introduce themselves.

3. **Expectations**–Share how the meeting will run and ask permission to facilitate: "I am here to help us get to the outcome we want. We may need to defer conversations that don't seem to be getting us to our outcome, are you okay if I need to interrupt conversations to keep us on track?" Ask the group if they would like to set any group agreements or ground rules to help them achieve the outcome.

The *midpoint* of a meeting uncovers the meaty information. Facilitating this part means turning the spotlight fully on the team. Let this section of your meeting develop as organically as possible.

Key roles of a facilitator here are:

1. Maintain ground rules.

2. Encourage team engagement as they generate ideas and solutions: read the body language and the speech tempos. Are they moving towards the outcome? Great! If not, can you change your state to help shift the room?

3. Capture and synthesize data if you have not assigned a note taker, either by asking, "who will capture that?" or by writing yourself. It is usually better to have the team write their own notes down but use your best judgement. As ideas get captured, group similar ones together to help spot trends that may emerge.

4. Keep the agenda on track. Help the team spot and defer conversations that do not support their

outcome. Call for regular breaks, in, "Why You Need to Unplug Every 90 Minutes," Drake Baer shares the research behind the performance degradation individuals see after ninety minutes.

5. Mark the meeting midpoint. In his book, *When,* Dan Pink explains that groups focus and work more urgently once they realize they have consumed half of the time allocated to their task.

The meeting *finale* wraps up the content of the meeting with a bow. Facilitators step into a more visible role and close the meeting on a high note. Have an exercise ready for participants to reflect on their results.

Key roles of a facilitator here are:

1. Orient your group on their journey during the meeting, what they accomplished and the decisions they made. Acknowledge the good work.

2. Validate next steps and commitments from the participants. Let them know what they can expect from you (notes, mentorship, recommendations) and ensure they left with clear rules of engagement for communication on the topic.

3. Survey the results of the meeting. Ask the team to give a thumbs up or down if they believed customers and investors would appreciate their work. Follow up with some individuals on their votes. These insights will help reinforce the outcome.

Beyond meetings, every project and product launch has a beginning, middle, and end. Communicating the key phases of a project helps teams gauge the effectiveness of their results. The beginning of a project is most uncertain and can seem filled with competing ideas and approach. Teams who use this time to effectively explore their most divergent ideas can create alignment around their solution that saves time when issues arise later in the project. Formally marking the midpoint of a project helps teams shift their focus to delivering their work on time. Finally, facilitators who have a plan around the end of a project (especially a big one) help their teams better transition into project maintenance and new work. This last part is significant because teams often feel their directions shift with neither the satisfaction of celebrating a completed project nor with plans for the inevitable remaining tasks and maintenance. Unaddressed, incomplete projects can create havoc on the estimation and execution of new projects.

READ THE ROOM

Facilitators take note of nonverbal communication, using it to "read the room" or gather clues on the team's state. This allows them to hear and see what others miss. Connect with the meeting's atmosphere by focusing on three distinct nonverbal areas: *body spacing*, *vocal tone*, and *engrossment*.

Often, individuals do not realize the messages they communicate because it occurs so subtly. Facilitators bring these messages to light, a practice which may label them as psychic, because those untrained in the methods of attuning to a group find nothing else with which to attribute their facilitator's insight.

Body Spacing

Humans bodies often still react like simple organisms—we draw in and move closer to that which attracts us, and we move away and lean back from what doesn't.

Facilitators use body spacing to understand what generates and what repels the group's energy. Discernment here is indispensable. For instance, if a facilitator sees the group quickly recoil and move away from a space, they can see it as a signal of a need to reestablish trust and safety, or as a moment of awe when an unbelievable new concept or design is revealed.

People who trust each other stand closer to one another (although leaders need a baseline to measure these shifts, as body space is cultural and physical closeness will differ from group to group). They can help create closeness in the room by moving in closer to the group members, but not so close where they feel uncomfortable. Due to the impossibility of calculating the sweet spot, this positioning sometimes requires trial and error.

Vocal Tone

Listen to the vocal tones of your teams. As a rule of thumb, remember this—deeper, slower-tempoed vocal tones signal grounded individuals, while higher, faster, and variable vocal tones show excitement. When a team becomes complacent, the quality of their voice becomes duller.

Use these clues to decide how to use your own vocal tone to guide the group dynamics. If you see teams losing energy, vary the tonality of your voice, and speed up your speaking tempo. When your teams need to focus, speak with a deliberately slowed pace and deeper tone.

Engrossment

Engrossment has a shape. Someone who is attentively listening looks different than someone who wants to speak or someone who is distracted. Individuals giving their full attention display *open* body language: relaxed, with their face, torso, and feet facing the person speaking. Individuals wanting to speak look rigid and tense. Distracted individuals look away from the speaker and fidget.

Watch the hands of group members. Though not precise, they can give us clues to the mood of individuals. Fists clench when someone experiences frustration and anger, whereas someone experiencing fear, anxiety, or trepidation may hide, wring, or tuck their hands away. Use these clues to cue into when to take a break or ask to defer a conversation.

MAKE IT THEIRS

Steve Jobs famously said, "it doesn't make sense to hire smart people and tell them what to do; we hire smart people so they can tell us what to do." Making it theirs means running a meeting so team members do exactly that: tell us what to do, rather than the other way around.

Conditioning makes it very easy for teams to rely heavily on their leader when faced with challenges. They often turn to the person who called the meeting to answer the questions on what they should do. When that happens, facilitative leaders throw the ball back in the team's court, and pose the question back to them for answers: "what do you think we should do?" Very quickly team members realize they have ownership in their meetings and its results. They ask each other for information to help solve the challenges and make decisions.

Facilitative leaders apply the practice of making it theirs to all of their meetings, even the ones designed to primarily convey information, like the quarterly earnings reports. They do this by asking their group questions or sharing stories. They can ask their group to spot trends on a chart. They can even ask the group to take a guess on what the organization's next steps should be given that information. Stories about team members create a lot of engagement, ie. "Chris wanted this change to happen for years now. Looking at these results, we may need to let Chris have an, 'I told you so' moment."

One more way of making it theirs is by sharing observations so that the team gains a holistic awareness of themselves functioning as a group. They may not realize that they keep circling back to the same topic, or that individuals squirm at the mention of a particular idea. These observations help create for the group what educators call a *meta moment*, or a space of awareness between what has happened and our reaction to it. This meta moment offers team members a chance to step back, connect the dots, and make better decisions.

SHIFT THE ROOM

Facilitators shift a room when they change the atmosphere of the meeting to one that invites more participation. In an age where brief attention spans rule the day, a facilitator's ability to shift a room is essential. By using what they learned from *meeting preparation*, as well as their *bodies*, *props*, and *breaks*, they can invisibly keep meetings on course.

Even with good structure and empowered attendees, meetings can slow down through friction, boredom, or disengagement. Conflict may even occur, yet conflict stems from the passion of the individuals in the group. Frustration only shows up when someone *cares* about a result, and they're not seeing it. Do not avoid conflict; instead direct the energy of the group to propel the work forward. Questions, such as "what solution would best reach the meeting's outcome?" or "what needs to happen in order to resolve this conflict?" could help direct the team's energy. Voting, or asking for a decider to make the decision, also helps resolve the conflict faster.

Use Your Meeting Preparation

When you prepared for the meeting, you learned more about the individuals on the team. Use that knowledge to lead the team in their process. Did someone show extra passion about the topic of the meeting? Call on them when the group's energy begins to lag. Beware of trying to make someone contribute what they shared in the interview. That won't help shift the dynamics of the meeting. Instead make it easy for that person to contribute if they would like to, but welcome all contributors to answer your question. Ask the group questions like, "why is this solution important?" and see if you can catch their eyes so they can answer. Their enthusiasm may give other attendees a new, more exciting perspective on the work.

Use Your Body

If Frito-Lay CEO Roger Enrico hadn't made effective use of his arms and body position in a meeting, his company would have missed out on an opportunity for one of the most lucrative product launches in its history. After inviting the entire staff to act like an owner of the company, a janitor took up the call and pitched a fresh new idea to Enrico and his board. Following the janitor's pitch, one of the executives in the meeting snarkily asked how much market share the janitor thought his idea would gather. Though unprepared for that question, the janitor smiled, held his arms outstretched, and said, "This much market share." Enrico jumped into action at the janitor's answer and stood up in the meeting saying, "ladies and gentlemen, do you realize, that we have the opportunity to go after that much market share?" and he too held his arms wide. This quick move from Enrico opened the door for the former janitor, now executive, Richard Montañez to bring his vision of Hot Cheetos to life—to the delight, pleasure, and red fingers of many.

Whether meeting with a five-person team retrospective, or a 100+ big room planning session, remember to use your physical body as a tool to command the group's attention. To start a meeting or important discussion, be official: widen your stance, straighten your posture, and add plenty of strength to your arms and hands. Not only are you telling the group what they will be doing in the meeting, you are also gathering attention back from the chit chat and side conversations that tend to fill a room when a meeting begins. Introduce the purpose of the meeting with plenty of vocal variety, à la TED talk style, letting your hands emphasize key points. These cues signal trust and show that the content of the meeting has substance and authority.

When the group is working together, nobody wants an overbearing, micromanaging leader, so lighten the formality of your facilitation here. When individuals share ideas, listen actively and use your body to communicate to others in the room what active listening looks like. Keep your hands open and loose. You don't need to take up so much physical space, so you can have your legs closer together. Decrease the "authority" in your voice because you are no longer telling your participants about their work: you are listening to their ideas and identifying connections and trends in what they are saying.

Sometimes you'll encounter larger or more rambunctious groups whose energy and passion can lead them down many rabbit holes. These groups may require more energy from facilitators, even when they are working together, so in this case you will need to widen your stance, keep your posture straight, and interject when the team has gone off topic. To calm down the group, lower your hands (by moving your hands palms down in a patting style). Bring attention back from side conversations using a lassoing movement.

Other times, you'll work with groups with low energy and participation. You can increase the energy in these groups by increasing the speed of your voice and body movements. Words like *what*, *now*, and *decide* stimulate answers. Furthermore, participants seated or standing in the corners of the room can get lost and disengaged. Help foster participation by speaking directly to all individuals throughout the meeting. In a big meeting, you may need to speak directly to groups of three to five, and facilitators may need to project or use a microphone to amplify the sound of their voice. These actions will cultivate collaboration. To invite even more collaboration, use hand gestures, like ones that signal "come over here" to foster inclusion, you aren't asking the participant to physically come over, but you are encouraging them to share their ideas with the group.

Use a Prop

At Atlassian, facilitators use rubber chickens to signal that an individual made their point and it is time to move on. In other groups, team members have a mascot, like a *b.s. Bunny* that they can throw when team members go down a rabbit hole.

Whether candy or buttons with pre-programmed sayings (like "that was easy"), props work wonders to change the mood of a meeting. They can wring out tensions and lighten everyone up. Props most often come in physical form but also in the nonphysical form of stories, questions, and jokes. Physical props carry symbolism or anchor a team's attention. Other meetings use time keepers with yellow or red signs to show how much time individuals have left. Some groups introduce talking sticks to help eliminate cross talking.

Stories can help make complex topics (and complex individuals) relatable. They can give authority to participants, sharing why they were invited and the skills they can contribute. Hearing real stories about the effects of the solution being worked on, and understanding the pain caused by not having a solution, can drive home the purpose of the work. Metaphors can also orient team members around what's happening in the meeting: i.e. "we're mobilizing our troops," "this is the home stretch," "hey, we're still on the field. This isn't half-time yet."

Questions can guide the scope, frame the context, and ultimately shape the architecture of the solution. The more detailed the question, the more it constrains the scope. Words used in a question matter; for instance, questions focused on stopping a problem may yield different outcomes than a question about fixing an issue. Much work has been published on powerful questions; however, a great facilitative skill is how to use them wisely. Sometimes less powerful questions are needed to keep a meeting flowing because a well-used powerful question could easily stop a team in their tracks. In their work, *The Art of Powerful Questions*, Eric E. Vogt, Juanita Brown, and David Isaacs share that a powerful question:

- » Generates curiosity in the listener
- » Stimulates reflective conversation
- » Provokes thought
- » Surfaces underlying assumptions
- » Invites creativity and new possibilities
- » Generates energy and forward movement
- » Channels attention and focuses inquiry
- » Stays with participants
- » Touches a deep meaning
- » Evokes more questions

The best powerful questions develop organically, from a deep curiosity about the work and the possibilities available to the team. Nevertheless, here are some great questions every invisible leader should have in their pocket:

» What part of what was just shared could be an assumption?

» Given our constraints, what *can* we do?

» What am I not asking that you really want me to ask?

Finally, jokes lighten the mood. Learn a new joke a week and see if any of them can appropriately help a meeting. Participants love to laugh, even at themselves. Some computer engineers love this one. "Some people say the glass is half full. Some people say the glass is half empty. Engineers say the glass is twice as big as necessary"—they even beam with pride when they hear it!

Use Breaks

Invisible leaders know when to call for a break. Well-timed breaks keep the team fresh and energized. If a group began swirling and rehashing the same fears, concerns, and worries, ask them to completely forget about the meeting for the length of the break. The group then reconvenes with sharpened focus and attention.

Breaks can also be utilized to get feedback on the meeting and engage different meeting leaders to take on different roles. If one person needs focused correction, at the break time pull them aside and use the time to connect with them, describing the specifics of what you observe. Ask them questions to uncover new possibilities. Some situations where focused correction is needed:

» They are not taking leadership that pertains to their role.

» Others stop talking or feel shut down when this person speaks.

» They are stuck and holding the team back.

If at any point your meeting escalates to a degree where you feel physical safety is in jeopardy, do not try to handle it yourself. Call in the support of office security, the police, or a professional trained in handling the situation.

Facilitative leaders can apply the principles of shifting a room to catalyze change in their day-to-day operations. When they see the energy of the office taking a slump, they can walk in with more energy, shoot someone with a Nerf gun, or gather the group for a fifteen-minute coffee break.

REFLECTING

Great facilitation looks like nothing happened at all
to create productive results. However, the truth is
that invisible leaders influence outcomes through
the foundational practices described: laying the
foundation, preparing, and conducting. Once they
deliver their intended outcomes, facilitative leaders
must spend some time on their own to reflect and
evaluate the effectiveness of their leadership, as well
as lead the reflection of others on the team.

Jack always has another meeting to get to, another product to launch, or another incident to manage. Frankly, he just doesn't have the time to reflect. Since he abhors participation medals, he only follows up when he does not like the outcome of his group's work. If asked, Jack would say that he's always neutral, and that a behavior like yelling at a group member is due to that individual's incompetence, not indicative of him personally. He also thinks it makes sense for him to do most of the talking, because he believes the group's best chance of success lies in listening to his directions.

Mariana knows that her reactions stem from a complex mix of her thoughts and environment, and that her best intentions can be sabotaged if she gets triggered by a group member. As a result, she forces herself to make time for reflection, and follows up regardless of a given meeting's outcome. If her group does not deliver the outcome she intended, she acknowledges what was lacking, and the work necessary to fill in the gap. If she finds that she spoke more than anyone else in her group, she reevaluates how she configured her team, and/or how well she was listening to them.

At its heart, reflecting is living the last principle of the Agile Manifesto, which reads, "at regular intervals, the team reflects on how to become more effective, then tunes and adjusts its behavior accordingly." In this chapter, we will cover how invisible leaders lead the reflection of others through **follow ups and acknowledgments,** as well as **deepening levels of listening** both during and after the meeting. We will also look at how invisible leaders reflect and manage their own emotions by **improving their instincts** and **resetting neutrality.**

As with all other tools in this book, there is no prescribed time to use the following techniques, but the sooner you follow up, the better. This helps keep information fresh.

German psychologist Hermann Ebbinghaus hypothesized that after learning something new, we forget forty percent of it within twenty minutes. After another forty minutes, we've forgotten half of it. One day later, we will have lost more than seventy percent. Though published in the late 1800s, his work is still referenced in popular books like *Make it Stick: The Science of Successful Learning* by Peter C. Brown, Henry L. Roediger III, and Mark A. McDaniel. Luckily, a simple ten minutes of review to practice any of the tools in this chapter within twenty-four hours of the learning can get learners back to almost 100% retention of what they originally learned. A week later, a mere five-minute review can bring back most of the learning. This helps keep everything learned in the meeting or workshop at the forefront of participant's mind.

FOLLOW UP AND ACKNOWLEDGE THE GROUP

Follow up and acknowledge the impact your group made. This can be done in an email or during a gathering, but you must first understand the exact impact the group made, what went well, what was learned, and how this ties into the broader organizational objective.

Sometimes our teams never get insight into how much their contributions affect the organization. As a result, individuals who take courageous actions may never hear if the risk was worth it. Be the leader who cares enough not only to say a generic thank you but to acknowledge how the actions affected the team. And, as in prepping, understand that you may need interviews or surveys to understand the full impact of what happened.

Example of a follow up message from Mariana:

Hi All,

I want to thank everyone for what turned out to be a very successful two-day PCI kick off. I think Pat said it best, "The two days felt like two weeks."

We uncovered a lot about ourselves and about each team. The biggest takeaway for me was that we all want to do our part to dramatically improve the safety of our customer's information *and* we will all need to readjust roadmaps to meet the challenge of this work. I am already seeing invites as follow-ups for action items we identified, which is a true sign of everyone's commitment to this mission. It is nice to have plenty of time to reset expectations on our other commitments for once.

I feel truly grateful to be working alongside such a talented group. Moreover, I think I can speak on behalf of the entire leadership team in saying that we are excited about the new structure you're creating to meet these demands. It was evident that this shift makes the most sense in order for our team to achieve the level of greatness we all desire. To that end, I really want to thank Pat, Cris, Micah, and Lee, for taking time out of their busy schedules (and for even rearranging travel) in order to join our offsite. The work we did was invaluable and just what we needed to move forward in the right direction.

Lastly, a huge, huge thank you to Lane and Cary for leading our workshops. We couldn't have done it without them.

Sincerely,

Mariana

P.S. Even with such a success, there is always room to reflect:

1. What can we learn from our workshop to improve on the Agile value of responding to change over following a plan?
2. You have clear roles and responsibilities! Before this meeting, no one interviewed *knew your roles.*
3. With the upcoming roadmap adjustments, you may want to brush up on your negotiating skills. William Ury, the cofounder of Harvard's Program on Negotiation, wrote in *The Power of a Positive No* that to help you create what you want, protect what you value and change what no longer works.

Follow ups are often neglected in the whirlwinds of new projects or other work. If you need motivation to follow up, note that *Harvard Business Review* identified lack of alignment, turf wars, and politics as the top barriers to innovation in a large company. A follow up does wonders to maintain the alignment of a group.

Furthermore, your messaging helps control the narrative around the work. Teams can do amazing things, but if their leaders fail to recognize them, their work can easily get lost, and leave others in their organizations deprived of opportunities to learn from their successes. Connect your group's work to the bigger picture and give them direction for their next steps, and you will find that this keeps them focused and in sync with the results you want to achieve.

DEEPEN YOUR LEVELS OF LISTENING

Listening at deeper levels changes us. It broadens our capacity to receive more information. It allows us to generate more flow in our meetings.

Often, the gems of a meeting lie in what was *not* said rather than what was said. How were other team members participating in the meeting? What type of listening did the group practice? Here are three common forms of listening in a meeting:

1. **Distracted Listening**– multitasking, and really not listening at all. At this level of listening, the conversation feels disconnected. Most communication is lost in the noise of the multitask.

2. **Self-Absorbed Listening**–patiently waiting for another person to stop talking in order to respond with your own point of view. At this level, the conversation feels rushed, and listeners may miss many nonverbal cues from the speaker.

3. **Connected Listening**–listening with full presence through everything others say and do. This level of listening flows; it creates space for new possibilities and highlights the said and the unsaid.

Connected listening is not only the goal for how a facilitative leader listens, but also how they'd like their group to listen to each other. Innovation hot spots require collaboration and the sharing of ideas. When teams practice connected listening, they consider the unique perspectives their colleagues bring rather than remaining entrenched in their own solutions. When a leader deepens their listening, they can identify when group members have created an echo chamber of ideas and invite the group to consider or find new ideas and perspectives. Reflect to see if any of the common traps are preventing connected listening in your meetings:

1. Falling for the Savior Complex. In *Wait, What*, James Ryan says, "the stance where you are the expert or hero who swoops in to save others." You selected your meeting participants because of their ability. Trust them to find their own solutions.

2. Becoming entrenched in only one solution. In his article, "Love the Problem, Not Your Solution," Ash Maurya writes that falling in love with your solution is the number one most common pitfall for entrepreneurs. Good solutions often emerge only after a messy process of lateral thinking and connecting seemingly unrelated ideas.

3. Getting caught up in past decisions. A meeting is a moving train. Regretting a past decision is doomsday for a facilitator because each decision you regret is time that removes you from what is presently occurring in the meeting. This is distinct from evaluating your last decision for its effectiveness and responding to the answer.

4. Focusing on what's wrong in the meeting. Focusing on thoughts like "people are not speaking up. People are on their phones. Participants are cross talking. Leadership is lacking" creates a hostile environment that no longer feels safe. Facilitators lose the opportunity to catalyze change when

seeing individuals as obstacles because they spend resources trying to fix them, instead of focusing on creating outcomes they want.

5. Experiencing the time crunch. A lack of time often moves individuals into self-absorbed listening. Meeting participants feel time-crunched when facilitators did not allocate sufficient time for the topic, nor did they pivot and renegotiate outcomes when information proved their time estimates incorrect.

6. Forgetting that connection is key. In the agile methodology, individuals and interactions are valued more highly than processes and tools. Stay connected to the individuals; break with expectations and conventions if it allows team members more ability to shine.

7. Forgetting to listen to themselves. An invisible leader focuses on how they listened to their own cues, and what subtler forms of communication their bodies were telling them. Did they have any gut-clenching, hair-raising, or fist-tightening responses that they didn't heed?

When facilitators reflect, their reflections are not tied to calendar events, but arise naturally out of their intention to do well by their teams. Therefore, they could (but do not always) reflect during their commutes, while grabbing lunch, while at the gym or running personal errands. In these moments, they think about further improvements to their leadership, and how to better respond next time they become ensnared in one of the common listening traps. For instance, if a time crunch caused self-absorbed listening, they may think of a way to handle that better in future meetings— perhaps by asking someone else to be timekeeper and time-boxing conversations to more disciplined limits.

IMPROVE YOUR INSTINCTS

Top leaders in any field often attribute their success to following their gut, and paying attention to their instincts. In facilitating work, instincts are crucial to identify subtle dynamics in the meeting. Unfortunately, in business, if listening skills are underdeveloped, embodied responses, like gut reactions, are often even more so. The following exercise can improve your awareness of your bodily responses:

Get very comfortable and watch a movie. Pay attention to how your body responds when the tension rises in the movie. Does your body tense up in any place? Does your breathing change? Understanding these biological cues allows for a faster identification when the tension in the team is rising.

Our brains are wired to mimic others; they create special brain cells called mirror neurons just for that function. Oftentimes, our bodies will display the traits of anxiety, such as shallow breathing and wringing hands, in response to someone else's uneasiness. When you can pick up these reactions in yourself, you can ask the group about it: "why am I feeling tension right now?"

RESET YOUR NEUTRALITY

If you found yourself decidedly unneutral during the meeting, practice a reset. What was your intended state? For instance, if you wanted to be patient, but repeatedly tensed up, you can devise relaxation exercises for the next time.

Build these good habits:

1. Be clear on the objective and commit to the outcome.

2. Build humility. Remember your group is there to come up with their own solutions.

3. Practice self-care, meditation, and good nutrition. It is much harder to stay neutral on a sugar crash.

4. Learn to like the people you are working with—all of them.

If those four ways to stay neutral do not produce neutral results, you may need to practice the neutrality reset process: The neutrality reset process must be done alone, and the steps are as follows:

1. Complain vocally. Release every single grievance. Be the biggest victim to other people and circumstances that you can be. Let out whatever words come naturally; use profanity if needed. Complain until you let it all out.

2. Once all the complaints have been voiced, notice how your body is reacting. Are your hands clenched? What about your jaw? Become mindful of the effects the complaints have led to.

3. Since you really don't want to be someone who complains or feels tense, start thinking about what

you do want, particularly in regard to the outcome you are striving for. Paint a picture of an outcome that excites you.

4. Once excited about the outcome, become clear on what you need to do to create the outcome you want.

TROUBLESHOOTING

As with most processes of the digital age, invisible leadership is cyclical, improving and adapting with each iteration. This chapter leaves you with action steps to handle the tricky parts of facilitation as you practice it in real-life situations. Remember, though described in a meeting situation, these examples can apply beyond meetings and be expanded to any part of the business theater.

SOME COMMON SCENARIOS (AND HOW TO ADDRESS THEM)

What if: Participants ignore one group member or individual

These patterns clue you into power dynamics that need neutralization. For generative dialogue and action to take place, all players need equal footing. If a manager contributes and the room turns silent, ask follow-up questions. If one group member's suggestions continually get lost in the conversation, pause and ask them to take in what the ignored person just said, ie. "one of you just shared, any comments?"

What if: Not everyone speaks in the meeting

Beware of letting your thoughts on what a good meeting *should* look like derail you from the meeting at hand. In the business world, you may often have meetings where not everyone speaks. Silence does not mean lack of participation, engagement, or leadership. An introverted genius may speak only once in a meeting yet completely revolutionize the work of the team. They may not speak at all, yet their faint nods of assent give other speakers the confidence to move forward with their ideas.

In this situation, watch the level of the team's *engagement,* their involvement in the task at hand. Observe their body language, like the position of their hands or the focus of their eyes. If the group isn't engaged, adjust the meeting to include small group break outs. Try a practice called Jigsaw, which assigns portions of the work to smaller groups of a large meeting, then have the group report their findings to the larger group and discuss.

What if: Someone dominates the meeting

When someone dominates the conversation, stand closer to them and make eye contact. These steps help most speakers become self-aware enough to realize they need to wrap up their point. If the individual continues to dominate, ask them to relate how it matters to the topic at hand, or if a timebox is needed. If the speaker does not heed the past steps, and proceeds to speak without allowing anyone, including you, a word in edgewise, you may need to get closer still. Try lightly laying a hand on the desk beside them, or on their chair, or, if it feels safe to do so, directly on their arm or shoulder. Be sure to listen to what they are saying, stay calm, and stand tall. Remember that your role is to help make the room a safe space for everyone, so do not create a battle of wills with the person, but do not continue with the meeting if it becomes unsafe. If the person continues to dominate, repeat what you are hearing and share that you will help them resolve the issue and pivot. Dismiss the group with the agreement to reconvene on the topic of the meeting at a different time and help the person.

How to: Remain authentic while setting context

Re-watch a movie or show that moved you. Watch the performers. Beneath their *sprezzatura* (the Italian word for their invisible artfulness), you can observe their tone, how they move their bodies, and their tempo for the subtle clues on how we move others towards specific outcomes.

Past seasons of shows like *American Idol* or *The Voice* can serve as another avenue to learn how to set context while remaining authentic. None of the finalists remains the same from first day to last, and the transformative journey showcases their work on controlling the context of their performance while remaining grounded in authenticity. If they can change from timid performers to megastars entertaining sold out stadiums, you can too (for your meetings).

What if: Individuals resist your facilitation

If there is a behavior that is being exhibited by multiple people in a group meeting, then it is absolutely effective to address one of them in front of the group. They then become the mirror for the rest of the group. To ensure the group understands the deeper meaning ask the group, "am I only coaching <name of the person in front of me>?" The group inevitably says, "no" and is able to take the lessons of the person being coached. This also lessens the vulnerability for the person being coached. Hot seats are uncomfortable, but if they know that they are "taking one for the team," it eases the burden. It also helps the group to bond.

What if: The meeting loses focus

During the middle of the meeting, a facilitator may need to address teams that have lost focus or need energy. If you asked for permission to facilitate at the beginning of the meeting, the team will respect you and allow you to get them back on their meeting journey. That is your value. They trust you to keep the meeting on track and focused. Here are some ways to do it:

Tie the conversation back to what they are discussing.

» "This topic clearly has a lot of <name emotion here> around it, let's rein it in so that everyone can speak and be heard."

» "We are spending extra time to delve deep into this item. What do we want to do with the other agenda items?"

» "How's the pace working for you? Will we cover and complete the next agenda items?"

Refer to an upcoming break.

Breaks involving food (like a catered lunch) are miraculous at creating ultra-focused and succinct groups.

» "How much time do you need? We'll break after this."

» "This is a tough problem to solve, and it is clear you have been problem-solving like crazy. Do you need a break?"

Use data.

» "We've spent fifteen minutes discussing this. We'll need to come to an agreement and we have ten more minutes before we adjourn."

» "Is this comment getting us closer or further away from the topic we are here to answer?"

Use observations.

» Does one person sometimes dominate? Repeating what the dominating person has said allows them to feel listened to, and more importantly, heard. Asking the person to listen for other points of view is also a great way to get them to focus back on the group.

» Has the topic become too heavy? Lighten the mood by telling a joke or noticing something outside of the story. Or even speak to the heaviness of the topic and ask if that's the reason you see the disengagement.

Make a request.

» "You walked in a little slowly. If today is a slow/low energy day for you, will this problem get the energy and passion it deserves?"

Evaluate yourself.

» Have you been talking most of the time? It is very hard for your group to engage in a topic and learn while being talked *at*. Always work to engage your group by talking less, asking more questions, and creating activities where they are writing. Ask a question.

» What has your mood been like? As a facilitator, your presence leads the team. If you have been sitting, slouching, or in any way broadcasting disengagement, it is time for you to shift. Set the context with your leadership.

» Are you mindful of addictions and cravings? Coffee, smoking, vaping, and texting generate dopamine hits that are difficult for the body not to crave. These dopamine hits are so strong, that, according to a study done at the University of Texas at Austin, just having a phone present in the meeting (whether it was on, off, in your purse, or right next to you), was enough to cause a decrease in a person's cognitive functions

What if: Participants are at an impasse

In the business world, years of CYA (cover your assets) mentality may have trained individuals to prefer pointing fingers over solving problems, resulting in lost information, missed deliverables, sore relationships, tension, and bad blood. When these groups get together in a well-facilitated meeting, they often discover their faulty assumptions. This can lead to an expansion of the problem statement that uncovers more work.

Sometimes, in order to move toward the objective, an old issue on the team must be aired out and resolved. When team members have been holding on to grievances for a long time, drama may result. Allow room for empathy because of the missed opportunities, hurt feelings, and limited possibilities.

Meeting objectives may need to change in the face of uncovering old issues. Ask the group to help reset expectations.

Leverage the well-respected leaders of the group to help guide decisions and next actions.

If the participants are at an impasse because they cannot agree on the decision, the following tools will help them move forward:

> » **Fist of five**–ask participants to score their agreement by raising their hands and displaying the number of fingers that signify their agreement on a scale of 1 (no agreement) to 5 (total agreement).
> » **Show Your Thumbs**–ask participants to share their agreement with a thumbs up, disagreement with a thumbs down, or disinterest with a thumb pointed to the side.

Ask the group how they want to address the data from the fist of five or show your thumbs exercise. Many times, this exercise alone helps the team decide on moving forward. However, if they cannot decide, ask the group to identify the decider, the person authorized to make the decision. If they don't know who that is, ask them to identify who would be responsible for the work affected by the decision, as well as who would be accountable for that work. If *you* are the decider, make the decision or negotiate when you will give an update to the decision.

Moderate behavior that gets out of line (like interruptions or use of constrictive language like "no, but") using hand signals similar to those used by traffic directors—when you want to have one person pause, put up your hand palm forward in a "stop" sign position. This will signal the person to pause (and believe it or not, it works!). You can then point to the other person who wanted to speak, and they will speak. Remind the group that there is plenty of time and space for everyone to be heard and considered and that the purpose of the meeting is to generate something together.

What about: Non-collaborative meetings, like all-hands meetings

All meetings can use facilitative leadership skills, especially all-hands meetings. The phrase "death by PowerPoint" didn't get invented by accident. Listening to an hour or two of technical implementations, key performance indicators, and budgets will easily zone your team out. These same steps that bring more punchiness to your collaborative meetings will add more zest to any meetings:

> » Tell a story that ties it back to the group, i.e. "remember when Ash didn't agree with this decision, but did it anyway? Well, look at these results."
>
> » Ask the group to answer a question, i.e. "what do you notice about where we were before this quarter, and where we are now?"
>
> » When asking for feedback, narrow the focus of the feedback, i.e. "what part of this plan might be the riskiest?"

CONCLUSION: BUILDING SKYSCRAPERS

The reader who takes the time to push their knowledge and understanding of how to make their teams better by making themselves invisible deserves a standing ovation for their courage, fortitude, and the impact they have on the business landscape of today. As with all great work, the fundamentals of invisible leadership are simple, but the application takes on infinite degrees of difficulty. It can be easy to question why to even do the work, when you may not get credit.

If that's what you're thinking, consider this: In his lecture on the birth of the skyscraper, Harvard professor Edward Glaeser describes the search for the inventor of the skyscraper as a fool's errand, because skyscrapers emerged as a collaboration of the leading architects working with each other. He goes on to state that "if anything, the city of Chicago deserves the credit, for it assembled a remarkable collection of architectural talent. . . . The skyscraper is a reminder of how cities solve their own problems . . . by enabling smart people to learn from one another."

Your efforts, likewise, enable smart people to learn from one another and leave a legacy of creative genius that emerged through laying the foundation, preparing, conducting, and reflecting on the work and their meetings. Building what could very well be the next round of skyscrapers, moon landings, and search engines for their business, their teams, and their consumers.

READING LIST

With much appreciation for their wisdom, this book cites from the following sources.

Adkins, Lyssa. *Coaching Agile Teams: A Companion for ScrumMasters, Agile Coaches, and Project Managers in Transition* (2010).

Allspaw, John and Evans, Morgan and Schauenberg, Daniel. *Debriefing Facilitation Guide* (2016). https://extfiles.etsy.com /DebriefingFacilitationGuide.pdf

Baer, Drake. Why You Need To Unplug Every 90 Minutes (2013). https://www.fastcompany.com/3013188/why-you-need-to -unplug-every-90-minutes

Brown, Juanita and Isaacs, David and Vogt, Eric E. *The Art of Powerful Questions: Catalyzing Insight, Innovation and Action* (2003).

Brown, Peter C. and McDaniel, Mark A. and Roediger, Henry L. *Make It Stick: The Science of Successful Learning* (2014).

Duhigg, Charles. What Google Learned From Its Quest To Build The Perfect Team. New York Times Magazine (2016).

Ebbinghaus, Herman. *Memory: A Contribution to Experimental Psychology* (1885).

Gates, Robert M. *Duty: Memoirs of a Secretary at War* (2014).

Goleman, Daniel and Boyatzis, Richard E. *Primal Leadership: Unleashing the Power of Emotional Intelligence* (2002).

Heath, Chip and Heath, Dan. *The Power of Moments: Why Certain Experiences Have Extraordinary Impact* (2017).

Kotler, Steven. *Rise of Superman: Decoding the Science of Ultimate Human Performance.* (2014).

Kotter, John P. *Leading Change* (1996).

Latino Leaders Network. Richard Montanez Honoree Remarks—LLLS March 11, 2014. YouTube. 13 March 2014. Web. https://www.youtube.com/watch?v=snCwpntpjmI&t=1679s

Liker, Jeffrey. *The Toyota Way: 14 Management Principles from the World's Greatest Manufacturer* (2004).

Maurya, Ash. Love the Problem, Not Your Solution. (2016). https://blog.leanstack.com/love-the-problem-not-your-solution-65cfbfb1916b

Ohno, Taiichi on the Toyota Production System. https://www.youtube.com/watch?v=ZK6vyFz7yrM&index=10&list=PLK1Sl3bHlnbji2dGE8NAQ7Nz8MZyQpMmc&t=150s. (2015)

Parker, Priya. We've Got to Stop Meeting Like This: Tips for Better Workplace Gatherings (2018). https://www.wsj.com/articles/weve-got-to-stop-meeting-like-this-tips-for-better-workplace-gatherings-1525447979

Peters, Thomas J. and Waterman, Robert H. *In Search of Excellence: Lessons from America's Best-Run Companies* (1982).

Pink, Dan. *When: The Scientific Secrets of Perfect Timing* (2018).

Ryan, James E. *Wait, What?: And Life's Other Essential Questions* (2017).

Sousa, David A. *How the Brain Learns, Fourth Edition* (2011).

Spangl, Jurgen. Want better meetings? Meet Helmut, the rubber chicken (2017). https://www.atlassian.com/blog/inside-atlassian /why-rubber-chickens-make-better-meetings

Stennett, Paul. "Ep. 005 Stacy Kirk: Using the Agile Method to Break Your Limits." The Transformation Blueprint, https://paulstennett.net /podcast/

Ury, William. *The Power of a Positive No: Save the Deal Save the Relationship and Still Say No* (2007).

Walsh, Bill and Jamison, Steve and Walsh, Craig. *The Score Takes Care of Itself: My Philosophy of Leadership* (2010).

Watkins, Alan. *Coherence* (2013).

Wellbourne, Theresa M. and McLaughlin, Lacey Leone. Making the Case for Employee Resource Groups (2013). https://onlinelibrary .wiley.com/doi/pdf/10.1002/ert.2140

ACKNOWLEDGMENTS

Just how *does* an author give proper acknowledgment to everyone who helped them create their book—and their first one at that?

Well, let me start with thanking my wonderful publishers at Sense & Respond Press: Joshua Seiden, Jeff Gothelf, and the wonderful Victoria Olsen. Smart, edgy, hard-working, you are gifts to the world. Anyone who gets a chance to work with you can call themselves lucky.

Thank you Alicia Carter, writing coach extraordinaire who fixed grammar and staid my frustrations. (She did not edit this section, all run-on sentences and passive voice are mine).

And thank you to all of my sweet support: Alejandra Marroquin, who on a balmy night in Caracas challenged me to stop criticizing books and start writing them. Ida Ferraz, who took me to the workshop that helped me believe I could write this.

Thank you to my coaches. Alicia, who I already mentioned but can never thank enough. Sandylu Guerrero, without you I could never have dealt with the messiness creativity brings (unpruned houseplants, stacks and stacks of paper, folded clothes left in laundry baskets and dirty clothes in a "pile" next to them). Kathryn LaBarbera, abundance and prosperity coach extraordinaire! Jerome Ware, without you, I would never have hired an editor, and this manuscript would have been lost inside a Google Drive drawer forever. And finally, to the best accountability buddy in the world, Sammy Gomez, every weekday, rain or shine, you are a model of responsibility and family.

Thank you alpha readers! Nadia Raizer, you always nodded and shared what worked (and gosh I needed that!). Daniel DiPasquo, you reminded me about the fold. Thank you everyone who asked about the book with interest, bright eyes, and big smiles.

Thank you to the very first invisible leaders in my life—my parents: Dina Ovalle and Arturo Astilleros.

And now humbly, I thank you, my reader. For learning, for being, and for leading. You make the world better.

ELENA ASTILLEROS is a coach, facilitator, and trainer who helps teams and individuals get the most out of their time. Using tools and best practices from Agile, Design, and Lean, Elena modifies them with techniques from coaching, facilitation, biohacking, and flow so that she can help teams uplevel when they are frustrated with their results and ready to increase their impact. Her high-performance toolkit stems from product delivery experience in roles with Ticketmaster, Toyota, Sony DADC, and the Hispanic Scholarship Fund.

www.elenaastilleros.com
🐦 **@ElenaAstilleros**
💼 **elena-astilleros**

Made in the USA
Coppell, TX
08 May 2020

24917722R00046